DOLLS & TOYS
AT THE ESSEX INSTITUTE

By Madeline & Richard Merrill
Photographs By Richard Merrill

Essex Institute
Salem Massachusetts

Essex Institute
Museum Booklet Series

© Copyright 1976 by the Essex Institute
Salem, Massachusetts 01970

Library of Congress Catalogue Number: 76-40405
ISBN 088389-066-6

Designed by Emily Hiestand Associates
Printed at Woodland Publishing Company

Publication expenses have been generously
supported by a grant from the
McCarthy Family Foundation
Charity Fund, Boston

Inside cover: *Horse-car pull toy of soldered tin, 1860-1880. Horses possibly made
by George W. Brown Company, Forestville, Connecticut. l. 24 in. (126,905A202)*

Foreword

The Essex Institute takes both pride and pleasure in initiating the publication of its vast museum collections with this booklet, *Dolls and Toys at the Essex Institute,* by Madeline and Richard Merrill. While many parts of these collections are well known and have been widely published by scholars, this new museum booklet series represents the Institute's first effort to bring the rich variety of its holdings to the public in comprehensive written form. Future books planned include furniture, silver, ceramics, prints, costumes, and textiles, among others.

Since they are among the best known and most intriguing exhibits in our collection, it is particularly appropriate that our fine dolls and toys be the first represented. No one is more qualified to write about them than Madeline Merrill, honorary curator of dolls, and Richard Merrill, who for many years has painstakingly photographed our many museum objects, including the irresistible dolls and toys in this book. Both are avid collectors. Mrs. Merrill is past president of the Doll Collectors of America and has worked with and lectured frequently on dolls for many years. We are especially grateful to the Merrills for their many hours of work on this manuscript and these fine illustrations. For her meticulous copy editing, Katherine W. Richardson of the Institute staff is also due our sincere thanks.

Furthermore, we are indebted to the trustees of the McCarthy Family Foundation Charity Fund of Boston for their financial support of this and other Institute publications. Their generosity has made it possible for us to begin to publicize and interpret our one hundred and fifty-five years of collecting the material objects of American society, and for this we are most appreciative.

Anne Farnam, *Curator*
Bryant F. Tolles, Jr., *Director*

The Essex Institute of Salem, Massachusetts, incorporated in 1848, is recognized as one of New England's oldest and finest historical societies, and among its varied museum collections is an assemblage of rare dolls and toys that span a period of over two hundred years. Of particular interest is the fact that so many are well documented and often have early Salem backgrounds. For instance there is a small-scale highboy said to have been made in Salem in the late eighteenth century (fig. 1), a barouche modeled after the first real barouche that appeared in Salem in 1822, and a wooden cradle painted brown and green with stenciled American eagles. The cradle was made by a British prisoner of war while being held on a prison ship in Salem harbor in the year 1812.

The collection as a whole is well known and justifiably so. It attracts the collector, researcher, historian, columnist, and author as well as the more casually interested grownup or the delighted child. Innumerable articles on the dolls and toys have appeared over the years in local and national periodicals, and many books published on the subject have included examples from the Essex Institute's collection.[1]

Although a limited number of serious collectors have always been interested in dolls, it was not until the mid-twentieth century that they attained proper recognition and stature as collectable objects. The *Christian Science Monitor* of 23 August 1974 reported that "dolls have become one of the biggest collection items in the United States — second only to stamps and coins. But model trains, boats, and any old iron or tin toys are also in big demand . . . ." Doll collectors have long known what today is an accepted fact — that the history of dolls parallels the history of the human race. They unerringly reflect their era and tell the history of man and his dress. The late Dr. Walter Hough, head curator of anthropology at the National Museum, Washington, D.C., stated that "the evolution of the doll is a very intricate subject.

Following the line backward one perceives that dolls lead quickly away from childish hands and become idols; representations in the sense of personations of spiritual or divinized ancestors."[2]

---

1. *"Emmeline," eighteenth century, "Queen Anne" wooden doll with a dress of the 1830 period; h. 22½ in. High chest of drawers, ca. 1790, with veneered and painted decoration; h. 22½ in., w. 12½ in., d. 7½ in. (125,088; 2,950).*

The greater part of the Essex Institute's doll and toy collection is displayed in the main gallery of Plummer Hall and in the Vaughan Doll House which is immediately behind the main building. The Gardner-Pingree House, designed by Samuel McIntire in 1804 and adjoining the Institute, also houses excellent examples of toys, dolls, and dolls' furniture in its third-floor nursery.

The Vaughan Doll House itself is a small historic building, measuring twenty-eight by sixteen feet. It has red clapboard walls, a high-pitched slate roof, and leaded-glass windows. The frame of the building is reputed to be from the first Quaker meeting house in Salem, built in 1688 by Thomas Maule. It was moved by the Essex Institute to its present location in 1865 and is one of the earliest examples of historic preservation in the country. It served as an exhibition building for museum objects in the 1870s and 1880s and played an important part in the development of the land surrounding Plummer Hall as other structures were moved or acquired by the Essex Institute. Since 1946 the Meeting House has been used as an exhibition space for the outstanding collection of dolls, children's toys, and furnishings — the gift of Mrs. Henry Goodwin Vaughan to the Institute. Today this charming house makes an imaginative and picturesque setting for her superb collection (fig. 2).

With the current surge of interest in miniatures the several doll houses at the Essex Institute receive much attention from visitors. The doll occupants, with their voluminous accessories and pieces of furniture, inhabit three large houses and some of the exhibition cases in the main gallery. Tea sets of eighteenth-century English creamware, Belleek, gold lustre, pottery, or Sandwich glass were an integral part of the proper miniature parlor, while a colorful little toy bellows might once have hung beside a small fireplace in an early doll house.

2. *Interior of the Vaughan Doll House in the back garden of the Essex Institute*

The Warren Doll House, one of the finest American doll houses known, has a rather plain three-gabled exterior which belies the elegance within (fig. 3). The house was made in 1852 by Israel Fellows, a Salem cabinetmaker, for the four daughters of Mrs. Annie Crowninshield Warren. With its elaborate furnishings largely intact, it is a perfect miniature of a mid-nineteenth-century merchant's townhouse. The little occupants of the house are contemporary in that they are, with the exception of one wax doll, enchanting little pegged wooden dolls of the early nineteenth century. Three of them, with their pegged-on china heads and limbs, are considered rare today by collectors.

Some fascinating stories about the house were provided by one of Mrs. Warren's daughters when she presented it to the Institute in 1925. The little mahogany drop-leaf table in the dining room was said to be part of a shipment of toys bound for India in a British ship which was intercepted and captured by a Salem privateer, Crowninshield's "America," in the War of 1812. Needless to say, the table remained in Salem, later becoming part of the Warren Doll House. The drawing room carpet was worked by Mrs. Warren to represent an Aubusson. Her expert needlework is carried out in the finest detail even to the monogram "W" worked on sheets, pillow cases, and table linen. Every effort seems to have been made to install all the essential fittings of gracious living in mid-nineteenth-century Salem.

Another historic doll house in the museum gallery has a mansard roof and was built by the cabinetmaker John W. Ayers for Bessie Lincoln of Salem in 1876 (fig. 4). She presented it to the Essex Institute in 1953 when she was eighty-five years old. The oak house is elaborately furnished in the revival styles that were popular in the late nineteenth century, including a handsomely carved parlor set in the Eastlake style. The house has been electrified so that every detail can be studied. Each Christmas it is decorated by the Ladies' Committee with Christmas trees, wreaths, garlands, and presents for every member of the doll family, and Santa Claus and his reindeer stand poised on the roof top!

Eighteen miniature dolls have a colorful home in an eighteenth-century-style shoe made by Mrs. Mary Luyster of Salem in 1858 (fig. 5). Mrs. Luyster meticulously created a delightful version of *The Old Lady Who Lived in a Shoe*, naming her "Dame Comfort." Dame Comfort's family includes six little pegged woodens with china heads and limbs, and six boy or men dolls, all of which are scarce by collectors' terms today. One of the men, probably the father, holds two babies in his arms while another gentleman "reads" a miniature book bound in red leather. Dame Comfort and Family came to the Essex Institute accompanied by a delightful poem, in which their creator describes and names each little occupant:

This is little Dame Comfort presented to you,
Another old woman who lives in her shoe,
But she never gives broth without any bread,
Or whips her poor children and sends them to bed;
But she teaches them how to be happy and good,
Pay respect to their elders and never be rude;
Be kindly affectionate one to another,
And never to tease little sister or brother;
To be ready at all times to set self aside
And check the first symptoms of passion or pride
To be early to bed and early to rise,
And pray every day to be harmless and wise
Thus little Dame Comfort with children eighteen,
Guides with discretion becoming a queen.

In her arms are the twins, little Neddie and Fred,
While Lucy and Tommy and Jane are in bed;
At the foot in the bath you will find Master Walter,
A second Tom Thumb, but decidedly shorter;
On the edge playing horse are Willie and John,
And Charles near his mother is full of his fun;
While young Master James, a pretty tall chap,
Holds Lilly and Daisy in state on his lap;
Little Fanny has slily crept out of bed,
And out of the toe she is popping her head,
To listen to Sydney reading aloud
To his good brother Dick about vapor and cloud
In full dress you'll perceive Miss Sophia and Ada,
The first in gold bracelets because she's the elder,
But one little maid in my hurry I've passed,
Her name is Helena, she stands near the bath.
1858 M.L.

5. *"Dame Comfort and Family," 1858, made by Mary Luyster; approximate h. of group, 6⅞ in., l. 11 in. (116,743).*

The range of dolls in the Essex Institute collection includes eighteenth-century woodens, as well as early twentieth-century bisques, homemade rag dolls and a good collection of paper dolls. Although they may not be clad in the clothing they wore when first purchased (since many early dolls have been redressed by succeeding generations), all the dolls are in the clothes they wore when acquired by the Essex Institute. Wood was one of the materials used for the earliest dolls. Plentiful and inexpensive, it has been used to a limited extent down to the present time. Eighteenth-century woodens, of English make, are among the earliest play dolls to be found today. Jointed and pegged, with brightly painted cheeks, pupilless glass eyes, dotted brows and lashes, and wigs of human hair or flax, they were made during the reigns of the British monarchs, Mary, Anne, and the Georges. Although commonly referred to by collectors as "Queen Anne" wooden dolls, they might more properly be called "Mary-Anne-Georgian" as they were made for well over a century and not only during the short twelve-year reign of Queen Anne.

During the eighteenth century, most dolls, including jointed and pegged woodens, were adult in form and dressed accordingly. Children's clothing resembled that of their elders also, and it is not uncommon to find portraits of the day showing little girls and their wooden dolls identically dressed as miniature adults. Unfortunately a doll that had been played with was often re-dressed as it passed down to later generations, and if necessary, bodily repairs were made. Several dolls in the Institute's collection remain as they were dressed by their last owners, and some have cloth or leather limbs, replacements for long-lost ones of wood. "Emmeline," an eighteenth-century wooden, illustrates such a doll (fig. 1). Her cloth limbs are replacements, but her glass-eyed wooden head and torso are in good original condition, as is her flaxen wig. She wears a cotton print dress of the 1830 period.

1. "Emmeline," eighteenth century, "Queen Anne" wooden doll with a dress of the 1830 period; h. 22½ in.

Particularly worthy of study is a finely preserved eighteenth-century "Queen Anne"-type jointed wooden doll, seventeen inches high.[3] Her brightly painted wooden head, with its pupilless glass eyes and stylized features, is in fine original condition, and even more unusual is the fact that she retains her wooden arms with their carved, forklike fingers. Her gown, probably dating from the early nineteenth century, is of embroidered mull and net over pink satin. While it is usual to find inset glass eyes on eighteenth-century wooden dolls such as these two, some had painted eyes. This is the case with another smaller "Queen Anne" wooden doll, about ten inches tall, documented as having been owned by Sallie Hill about 1800. She wears an early dress and her little owner made her hat.

Perhaps the most transformed doll in the collection is a quaint "make-do" doll, a much-battered and scarcely recognizable eighteenth-century "Queen Anne" wooden doll. Originally fair-haired and light-complexioned, she was painted black, probably between the years 1840 and 1860, to represent a Negro. She now wears a curly black yarn wig and is clothed in a brown print dress and checked apron (fig. 6). She has a charm of her own and attests to the ingenuity and frugality of an earlier age.

6. *"Queen Anne" doll, eighteenth century, wooden with replacement cloth limbs. She has been painted black and re-dressed at some point in the mid-nineteenth century, 1840-1860; h. 16 in. (114,022).*

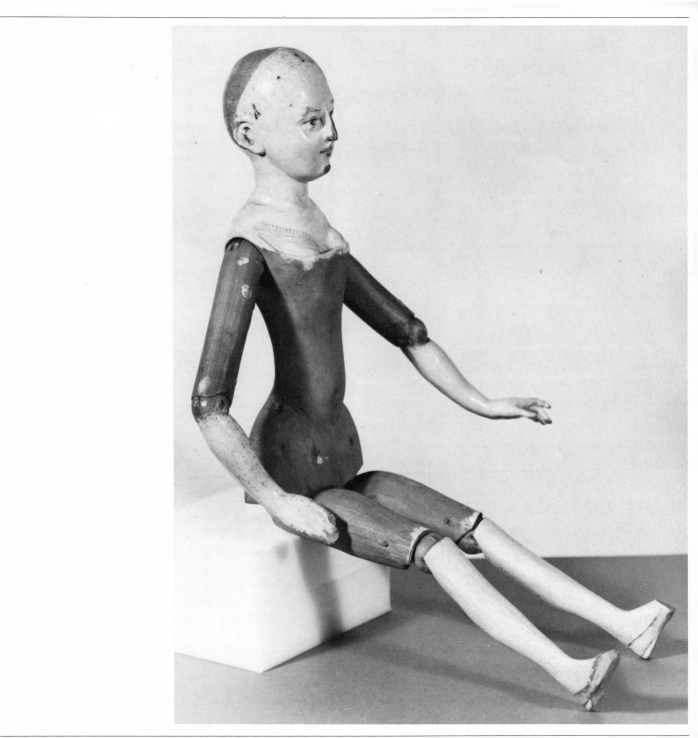

The fine craftsmanship found in early eighteenth-century wooden dolls may be seen in one that was brought home to America before 1797 by Nathaniel Archer of Salem (fig. 7). A well-proportioned lady doll, she has a carved wooden bodice, painted features, deeply carved ears, and a black-painted pate which was once covered by a nailed-on hair wig. Her waist is long, slim, and curving, and the joints of her limbs are of the ball-and-socket variety. The interesting body structure may be seen to advantage, as she is displayed undressed.

Seventeenth- and eighteenth-century jointed wooden dolls were generally more sophisticated and more skillfully made than those of a later date. By the early nineteenth century their quality had considerably lessened, a trend which continued throughout the nineteenth and into the early twentieth century, when they ceased to be made commercially. At the end, they were so crudely turned out that they bore little resemblance to their far-removed and finely carved predecessors.

Four rare and unique French dolls of about 1800, with heads and knee-length torsos of carton moulé, are still attired in their original Directoire costumes (fig. 8). Three of these dolls, ranging in size from nine to twelve inches, are rudimentary in construction, having stick legs attached to square wooden bases and flat, flipperlike wooden arms tacked to the shoulders. The expressions on the faces of this rakish-looking threesome are rather crudely drawn, and as they unbendingly stand in their tattered gauze and paper dresses, there is a certain air of jauntiness about them.

The fourth and largest of the group, standing slightly over sixteen inches in height, is better proportioned and of higher quality than the others. Her shapely wooden legs have feet of plaster, and her wooden arms, in a bent position, have hands with forklike fingers. Her well-preserved head has nicely painted features with a serene expression, in contrast to the other three. Her Directoire costume of pink paper, white satin, and gauze is trimmed with a fringed gold braid. In addition to the white

7. Lady doll, eighteenth century, wood, undressed, showing the finely detailed hand carving. By tradition the doll was brought to Salem before 1797; h. 24 in. (109,672).

8. Four French dolls of the Directoire period, ca. 1810, carton moulé and wood with painted features and paper and gauze clothes; h., left to right, 13 in., 12 in., 9½ in., 17½ in. (1,873.1 - .4).

cap she wears, she holds in her left hand a gold-trimmed, white "collection hat," and from it is suspended a golden cord with a metal bell.

These four dolls of the Directoire period are of the type shown in the 1804-1814 toy catalog referred to as the "Maury Album." This album was colorfully reproduced nearly a hundred years later by Henri D'Allemagne in his book, *Histoires des Jouets*, published in Paris in 1903. The dolls were made as inexpensive playthings, and they and their clothing are extremely fragile. It is not surprising that few are known to exist outside those in the Essex Institute's collection.

In the beginning of the nineteenth century inexpensive little pegged wooden dolls became popular, and they continued to be made until the middle of the century. Those made through the 1830 period have yellow-painted wooden combs atop their heads and wear dresses with the high-waisted styles of the Empire period. "Henrietta," a pegged wooden doll of 1820 (fig. 9), has just such a yellow wooden comb in her smooth black carved hair, and wire loops, which once supported earrings, are imbedded in her ears. Her early costume consists of a high-waisted gauze-and-net dress sashed and trimmed with pink ribbons. Dolls such as "Henrietta" are referred to as "tucked-comb" wooden dolls by collectors today. They were the type played with and dressed by the young Princess Victoria, and they may be seen pictured in delicate watercolors in *Queen Victoria's Dolls*, a book published in London in 1894. Wooden dolls made after 1840 have low waists and no painted combs.

Dolls with heads of papier-mâché appeared on the market shortly after the first decade of the nineteenth century. Papier-mâché is made of paper pulp mixed with sizing, paste, resin, and other materials, and when molded and dried it becomes hard and durable. Dolls with heads of this material vary greatly in model and size. Generally French- or German-manufactured, the heads have glass or painted eyes, molded or real hair coiffures, and may come with bodies of wood, cloth, or leather. It is often difficult to determine whether a doll head made in the last half of the nineteenth century is of papier-mâché or composition as the latter is basically papier-mâché with mineral additives.

The erroneous and misleading term "Milliner's Model" is often attached to dolls with papier-mâché heads mounted on wooden-limbed bodies of leather or cloth. Made during the first half of the nineteenth century, they are generally small in size, and their molded coiffures, often elaborately styled, are carefully detailed. Perhaps the term "varnished heads," a name given to them in German toy catalogs at the time of their manufacture, would be more correct as a collector's term.

The production of papier-mâché dolls was great, as was their variety. Two of the several examples in the Essex Institute collections are the much-appreciated twins, large dolls of the mid-nineteenth century, whose identical garb includes orange-and-white print dresses, printed velvet jackets, and wide-brimmed hats of beaver and silk. Also there is "Frances Ann" who has the usual wasp-waisted kid body with wooden limbs. She was brought to Salem in 1846 and still wears her original printed dress and hat of straw.[4]

9. "Henrietta," ca. 1820, jointed wooden doll. Her painted head has a yellow wooden comb; h. 9 in. (125,073).

A papier-mâché doll, whose finely detailed head has a classical look, was once the plaything of Mary Narbonne of Salem, and is one of several in the collection with an interesting Salem history (fig. 10). Salem vital records list Mary Narbonne as being born on 23 May 1824 in the seventeenth-century Narbonne house on Essex Street. Her doll is of the 1820-1830 period, and her painted-and-molded hair has a braided coronet and comb on top. She wears a plain white high-waisted dress with long sleeves and a blue sash.

Another small doll, dressed as a girl of the late 1830s or early 1840s, was given to Rebecca B. Manning, a cousin of Nathaniel Hawthorne, by her roommates at the Ipswich Female Academy (fig. 11). The little doll wears a blue-and-white print dress which is full-skirted, tightly waisted, and has short lace-trimmed sleeves. Following in the girls' style of the day, cotton pantalettes caught at the ankles show well below the much-shorter dress. A broad-brimmed hat of natural straw with white ribbon ties completes her costume.

"Anstiss Derby" was said to be a "fashion doll" when she was brought to Salem in 1826 for Martha Pickman, daughter of Benjamin and Anstiss (Derby) Pickman and granddaughter of Elias Hasket Derby (fig. 12). Miss Pickman had the stylish French doll's dress copied as her own first ball gown. The doll, "Anstiss," has a papier-mâché head with an extremely thin coating of wax, brown glass eyes, kid body and arms, and wooden legs. Her elaborately dressed wig of real hair is entwined with pink roses. Her dress of blue silk, now much faded, is trimmed with metallic braid. She came encased in her original wooden box with a sliding cover.

---

10. Papier-mâché doll, with wooden body and limbs, 1820-1830, was owned by Mary Narbonne of Salem; h. 12 in. (130,314).

11. Papier-mâché doll, dressed in the style of 1830-1840. She was given to Rebecca B. Manning by her classmates at the Ipswich Female Academy; h. 8¾ in. (121,506).

12. "Anstiss Derby" has a wax-coated papier-mâché head and wears her original stylish ball gown. She was brought to Salem about 1826 for Martha Pickman; h. 14½ in. (129,202).

"Sarah Ann Phippen" is a large French papier-mâché doll who is clad in a plaid silk dress made from the wedding gown of Mrs. Martha C. Phippen (fig. 13). A fine doll, with an all-kid body, "Sarah Ann" dates from the second quarter of the nineteenth century and has set-in glass eyes, an open mouth showing teeth of split bamboo, and a wig of dark brown human hair. She also wears pantalettes, and her low leather shoes are green. Another large papier-mâché doll is illustrated in figure 14; largeness gives this doll added interest as most dolls of this type (the so-called milliners' models) are much smaller in size.

In 1858 the first doll patent in America was granted to Ludwig Greiner of Philadelphia for a reinforced head of papier-mâché. Ludwig Greiner emigrated to America in 1830, and it is thought that he was a skilled maker of doll heads at that time. One of these early patented dolls is part of the Vaughan Collection and is displayed in the Doll House (fig. 15). As is usual with Greiner dolls, her features are painted, including her eyes, and her hair is molded. The 1858 Greiner label is still intact on the lower edge of the back shoulders. Her body is cloth with leather arms, and she wears a full-skirted, red print dress with a lace-trimmed white collar. Her leather shoes are handmade.

13. "Sarah Ann Phippen," a French papier-mâché doll, 1825-1850; h. 28½ in. (118,162).

14. Detail of a papier-mache headed doll, ca. 1840, showing molded hair and delicately painted features; h. 25 in. (126,905a.133)

15. Detail of doll with a papier-mâché head patented by Ludwig Greiner, 1858; she still bears her original label; h. 29 in. (126,509a.227).

Dolls were not made commercially in America until around the middle of the nineteenth century, and even then the percentage of American-made "store" dolls was small in comparison to those imported from England, France, and Germany. Therefore one must keep in mind that most dolls found in museums and collections are of European origin. Germany, where doll making had flourished since medieval times, dominated the field until World War I interrupted trade. At this time Americans stepped up the manufacture of dolls as well as importing some from Japan. From this time on, American production increased steadily, and today American children play almost exclusively with American-made dolls.

From the earliest days in America, however, countless numbers of homemade dolls have been created out of cloth, leather, or whittled wood by elders for their children and grandchildren. In proportion to "store-bought" or imported dolls, few have survived. The majority were discarded as not being worthy of preservation, or may have been literally used up by love and play. Classed now as primitives, these once-lowly dolls are extremely well regarded today, not only by doll collectors, but also by those interested in American folk art. Being handmade, no two are exactly alike. Some are finely executed while others are crudely made, the degree of workmanship depending entirely upon the skill and ingenuity of the maker. Their everyday work attire, generally of cotton cloth, reflected their modest station in life.

Of humble origin is a crudely carved wooden doll which evokes much comment from visitors to the Essex Institute (fig. 16). An aged woman, she has a stern visage with long nose, sharp chin, and painted wrinkles. Remnants of a once-white wool wig cling to her elongated head. Her wooden body, with the exception of cloth arms, is of one piece from the top of her head to her jointless stump legs. While there is no proof of her age, she was probably made in the mid-nineteenth century. She wears a simple blue-and-white print dress under a blue-and-white checked apron. Another colorful character is

"General Stark," whose crudely whittled head of wood is mounted on a thickset white leather body. Possibly he was made by a patriot who lived in the time of the Revolutionary War hero, but regardless of his age, the general projects a strong and manly image.[5]

Dolls of cloth, along with those of wood, date from very early times. Many are of great charm; created at home from easily available fabrics, these dolls fall into the category of early American primitives. There is a busily knitting old dowager, seated in her own small easy chair, who was made by Miss E. Kimball of Salem about 1785. She wears her original straw poke bonnet, but her present black silk dress is a replacement of 1863. Two quaint old rag dolls, much played with and loved, judging by their appearance, certainly fall into the primitive class (fig. 17). Their features and hair, now badly faded, were originally drawn in black ink. Their arms and legs end at the wrists and ankles. The lady, dressed in a plaid skirt and underwear, has probably lost the upper part of her dress. The man's outfit is quite complete, consisting of a long blue coat, striped homespun trousers, shirt, black silk tie, and a brocade vest.

16. *Handmade wooden doll with cloth arms, mid-nineteenth century; h. 12 in. (107,210).*

17. *Handmade rag dolls, mid-nineteenth century. Their faded features were originally drawn in ink; h. 12½ in.; h. 12 in. (114,143; 114,144).*

A knitted black doll, having great verve, was made in 1892 by Mrs. Sarah Kimball when she was seventy-eight years old (fig. 18). She is gaily dressed in a red, white, and blue knitted costume which includes a smartly styled sailor hat. In the same year, 1892, *Harper's Bazar* carried instructions for making a similar knitted boy doll. Directions were given not only for completing the doll and costume, but also for the shaping and stitching of the ears, nose, facial features, and hair: "work two eyes and eyebrows with black sewing silk and lips with red. Sew on brown worsted in little curly rings for hair." The long detailed instructions ended, "this is an absolutely reliable set of directions." And judging from the doll made by Mrs. Kimball, such directions were indeed all of that.

Wax, along with wood and cloth, has been used in the making of dolls from ancient to modern times, and during the nineteenth century a great variety of wax dolls were made. Their declining popularity at the end of the century was a trend that continued into the early years of the twentieth century, when their production finally ceased. Although some wax dolls were made in France, most originated in England and Germany. Wax dolls were both poured and dipped, and one of the latter type in the Essex Institute collection is said to have been the first wax doll in Salem. Another, "Hope Richardson," is named for the child who owned her about 1857. She has rosy cheeks, brown glass eyes, and a human hair wig, and she is dressed in her original peach-colored silk dress and cotton pantalettes.[6] Any doll with a molded-on bonnet or hat is always of interest to collectors, and a few of the dolls with dipped or wax-over-composition heads are found with this feature, such as a lady doll whose partial hair wig, caught in a snood, peeks out from beneath her molded-on pink bonnet.[8]

A child doll of highest quality has a realistically modeled poured wax head with set-in glass eyes and inserted hair, brows, and lashes (fig. 19). She was probably made during the third quarter of the nineteenth century by one of the famous families of London wax doll-makers, such as Montanari,

Pierrotti, or Marsh. Poured wax dolls by these makers are known for their beauty and fine detail, although most are unmarked. The doll's hollow limbs are also of poured wax, and her body is of stuffed cloth. She wears a print dress of sheer cotton fabric.

---

18. *Knitted doll made by Mrs. Sarah Kimball in 1892. Her dress is red, white, and blue; h. 16 in. (102,915).* Opposite

19. *Child doll, poured wax with set-in hair, brows, and lashes, third quarter of the nineteenth century; h. 18 in. (120,807).* Right

A doll that is seldom seen today is the "London Rag Baby," whose cloth-stuffed head has a wax facial mask covered with tightly drawn gauze (fig. 20). Advertised as "London Rag Baby Dolls with muslin covered wax faces, prettily painted, with hair. Can be thrown about without damage or risk to furniture," they were made in England during the last half of the nineteenth century. This particular baby doll once belonged to Mrs. Robert W. Willson and while her white-lace-trimmed and ruffled bonnet is original, her long printed cotton dress is a later addition.

When Mrs. Joshua Dodge of Salem returned from a trip to Paris in 1838 she brought with her an elaborately costumed wax doll (fig. 21). Although purchased in Paris, the doll was probably made in Germany, and it looks as if it had never been played with. Her round wax-over-papier-mâché head has glass eyes and a curly mohair wig with a tulle bow, and she has a cloth body with pink kid arms. Her original mull dress, once pink, has a laced white satin bodice with puffed sleeves and a skirt trimmed with three rows of ruffled tulle. Her collars and cuffs are edged in appropriately delicate lace.

Six exquisitely costumed wax ladies are encased in their original paper-lined, glass-paneled wooden box (fig. 22). They are reputed to have been brought back to Salem from Portugal by Captain James Cheever in 1795. The little figures have heads and arms of wax, and their wooden legs end in carved high-heeled, pointed-toed shoes. There is a haughtiness in the expressions of their long waxen faces, and despite their small size they are regal in appearance. Each doll has her own blue-painted wooden stand, and the costumes, with matching hats, are of varied colored silks, elaborately trimmed and finely detailed in a late eighteenth-century court style.

20. "London Rag Baby," cloth stuffed head with gauze-covered, waxed facial mask, second half of the nineteenth century. The doll wears her original bonnet, but the dress is a replacement; h. 17½ in. (122,422).

21. *Doll, probably German-made, with wax-over-papier-mâché head brought from Paris by Mrs. Joshua Dodge in 1838; h. 20 in. (2,383).*

22. *Six wax dolls in their original case, said to have been brought from Lisbon, Portugal, by Captain James Cheever in 1795; h. 10 in., w. 19 in. (3,721).*

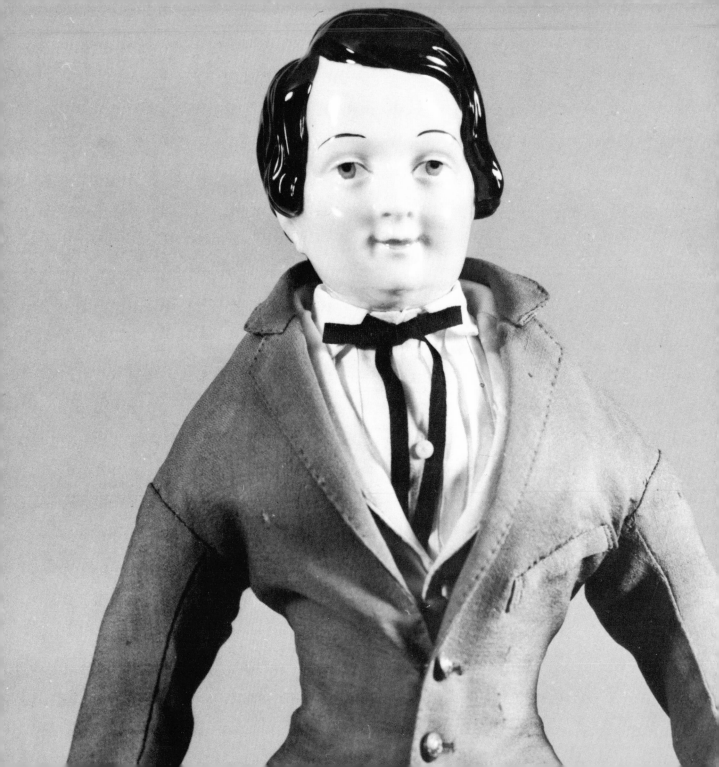

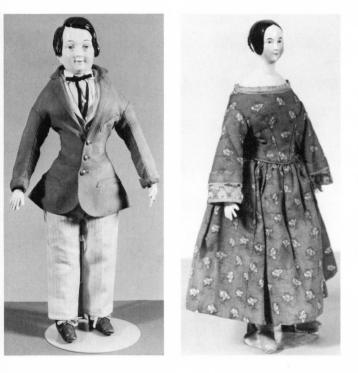

Dolls with glazed ceramic heads, called "chinas" by American collectors, first became popular in the 1840s, and as is true of many other types of dolls, the earliest are the finest. Most china-headed dolls were made in Germany, but a limited number were also manufactured in France. They usually have black molded hair, blue-painted eyes, and are generally unmarked by their manufacturer. Rarities among china-headed dolls include those with brown molded hair or real hair wigs; brown painted eyes or inset glass eyes; swivel necks; and china head, arms, and legs pegged to a jointed wooden body. A head marked by one of the famous European porcelain factories — K.P.M., Royal Copenhagen or Dressel, Kister, and Company — is also extremely rare and when found on a man doll (fig. 23), it is especially prized by collectors. The marks of the Konigliche Porzellan Manufactur of Berlin appear on the inside shoulders of this young man, who has finely molded brown hair and a deep pink-toned face with painted blue eyes. His original hand-stitched clothing is finely tailored down to the last detail, including his linen underdrawers and a small pocket handkerchief. "Lucy," a fine French china-headed doll in the collection, has a blond mohair wig and blue-painted eyes. In addition to the clothes she wears, she has an extra wardrobe all in the latest French style of 1870, the year in which she was brought to Salem.[7]

A sensitively molded little china-headed lady doll, of the 1840-1850 period, has a cloth body and leather arms (fig. 24). In contrast to "Lucy" or "Marie" (see fig. 30), her dress looks homemade, the fabric appearing too heavy in weight for a small doll's dress. Perhaps it matched her young owner's dress, or was made from a scrap of fabric left over in the sewing basket. Its style and fabric, however, match the era of the doll's manufacture.

23. Man doll with china head, made by Konigliche Porzellan Manufactur, Berlin, Germany, mid-nineteenth century. He wears his entire suit of original clothes; h. 19½ in. (126,905a.81).

24. Lady doll with a china head, 1840-1850. Her brown molded hair has a braided coil in back; h. 12 in. (4,149b).

Another small doll, "Alice," is a particularly unusual china-headed doll, with her set-in glass eyes and human hair wig, two features that are seldom seen in dolls of her type (fig. 25). Her glass eyes are deep blue in color and have painted upper and lower lashes. Her body is cloth with leather arms, and she is simply dressed in printed cotton.

Large dolls are found in all materials, including china, and they seem to attract much attention, especially from children, perhaps because they appear so lifelike and close to their own size. Several large dolls, including a fine china-headed one (detail, fig. 26), are arranged in the Vaughan Doll House as if they were children at play in an old-time nursery (see fig. 2). Another large china-headed doll was donated to a fair in Salem about 1875 (fig. 27). Her full-skirted sheer cotton dress, banded in a narrow red ribbon, may have been made for the event.

There are two dolls in the Vaughan collection who are dressed in Quaker costumes, and their heads, one papier-mâché, the other china, have been appropriately chosen by their original owners for their quiet ascetic look. The china-headed doll (fig. 28) has a most fittingly serene expression as she reads her tiny book. She is a handsome doll in her complete Quaker garb, which consists of a gray satin dress and bonnet, hemstitched kerchief of white linen, finely made underclothing, white stockings, and handmade leather shoes.

25. "Alice," mid-nineteenth century, has a china head with set-in glass eyes and human hair wig; h. 13 in. (125,096).

26. Detail of a china-headed doll whose molded hair is caught up in a painted snood, mid-nineteenth century; h. 30 in. (126,905a.225).

27. *Doll with china head, cloth body, and leather arms, dressed for a fair in Salem, 1875; h. 28½ in. (105,254).*

28. *Doll with china head, mid-nineteenth century. The doll has been dressed as a Quaker; h. 20 in. (126,905a.101).*

The golden era of dolls began in the 1860s when bisque-headed dolls, with both tinted and untinted complexions, began to appear on the market. The early untinted bisques are often referred to as "parians." Such heads, of invariably high quality, have delicately tinted features and usually have molded hair rather than wigs, glass or painted eyes, and, occasionally, pierced ears. The most elegant ones are elaborately embellished with a variety of molded or painted hair ornaments, scarves, collars, guimpes, vests, ruffles, or bows. For instance, one small choice parian doll in the Institute's collection has blue-painted eyes and long, molded blond curls. Her cloth body has parian limbs which include her booted legs, partially glazed and trimmed with gold lustre.[8] "Lulu" has a parian head with set-in glass eyes and pierced ears, and her elaborately dressed, molded blond hair is banded in a narrow black ribbon (fig. 29). A white square-necked, molded guimpe completely covers her shoulders under her clothing, and a brown-painted ribbon with a gold-and-crimson locket encircles her neck. She has a cloth body and wears a cotton dress of blue-and-white check. She also has a long, hooded cape of dark blue wool.

Although a few early bisque dolls may have been made, the material was not popular until the 1860s and 1870s when the French produced the artistically made, lavishly costumed bisque-headed lady dolls now called "French Fashions" or "Parisiennes." They were superseded in popularity by the bisque-headed child doll and baby doll in the late nineteenth and early twentieth centuries. The French child dolls, with sensitively modeled heads of the finest bisque, came beautifully attired in the latest French styles. Called "Bébés Incassables," they and the "French Fashions" or "Parisiennes" are avidly sought by collectors and today are considered to be the ultimate in beautiful dolls.

29. "Lulu" has a parian head and set-in glass eyes. Her molded blond hair has been elaborately coiffed. Late nineteenth century; h. 18 in. (125,091).

The majority of bisque dolls were made in Germany and France, and competition between the two countries was keen. By the end of the nineteenth century, Germany dominated the market and continued to do so until World War I, when production was temporarily halted. During this period some bisque dolls were made in Japan and America, but following the war they were again made and exported by Germany. However, the demand for them had so diminished that by the early 1930s they ceased being manufactured. The total production of bisque dolls was enormous, especially in Germany, so that they are still easily available to collectors today.

The early bisque-headed "French Fashions" or "Parisiennes" came dressed in the latest Paris fashions and often had trunks and suitcases filled with complete trousseaus. At times it has been erroneously stated that these dolls were used as fashion mannequins, but this is not usually the case; they are fashionably dressed play dolls, luxury items made for well-to-do children, and they reflect the great wealth and consumer economies that developed in many countries at the end of the nineteenth century.

Occasionally, however, the costumes on these dolls were so highly styled and finely made that individual dress makers were influenced by them. "Leonide," a fashionably dressed, bisque-headed lady, was brought from Paris to a young girl in Salem in the 1870s, and it is said that her gowns were so admired that a leading Salem dressmaker copied them for her clientele. The little trunk which accompanied her contains walking and traveling suits, morning and evening gowns, hats, trinkets, and an assortment of various fashion accessories. Perhaps few dolls in the Essex Institute collection are more admired than "Marie," brought from Paris about 1870 to Mary Crowninshield Endicott, whose initials are on the doll's trunk (fig. 30). "Marie" arrived with a wardrobe that would be the envy of any well-dressed child or woman: four dresses, three capes, five skirts, several blouses, two jackets, five hats, two bonnets, several pairs of shoes, a shoe horn, nightgowns,

30. *"Marie" has a bisque head and arms and a kid body. She was brought from Paris about 1870 for Mary Crowninshield Endicott. She is surrounded by her many possessions; h. 14¾ in. (127,424).*

32. *Doll with a rubber head, mid-nineteenth century; h. 18½ in. (107,242).*

underclothing, and plain, striped, and lace stockings. She has her own corset and bustle, combs and brushes, jewelry, fans, and pocketbooks. She travels with a valise, hat boxes, and traveling rug, or takes her trunk. At home she can write letters, sew, play cards, or read, using her own eye glasses. Marie watches the opera with her lorgnette and the horse races with field glasses. She even owns several pieces of furniture, including a chaise longue on which to relax, perhaps made for her after her arrival in America.

A fine German bisque doll made by the firm of J. D. Kestner, Jr. was given to Ella Low of Salem in 1891 (fig. 31). She exemplifies many of the bisque dolls of the later period. She has a socket head with moving glass eyes, an open mouth with teeth, and a human-hair wig. Her composition body is elastic-strung and she is dressed in the full-collared style of the 1890s.

While bisque, china, papier-mâché, and wax were the predominate materials used for making dolls, the nineteenth century was also an age of experiment, when two other materials, gutta percha and rubber, were used as well. Dolls with heads of these materials appeared by the 1850s and are relatively scarce today. The Institute collection contains a large fine rubber-headed doll[9] and one of smaller size (fig. 32). Paper dolls were also popular and have been made for centuries. With the improvement of printing technology in the nineteenth century, their numbers grew to great proportions. The Institute has a good collection of paper dolls, including one of Jenny Lind[10] and one of Mrs. Tom Thumb, but the subject will not be elaborated on here, as it could easily fill another volume.

---

31. Doll with a bisque head, given to Ella Low of Salem in 1891. Made by J. D. Kestner, Jr., Germany; h. 16½ in. (132,144.1).

Mechanical dolls and toys intrigue young and old alike today, and one can imagine the thrill a youngster must have had in the mid-nineteenth century when a doll walked by herself, pushed a cart, or rowed a boat. The "Autoperipatetikos," or walking doll, has in her cardboard conical body a key-wound clockwork which enables her to walk on somewhat clumsy metal feet (fig. 33). She has a china head and kidskin arms and is labeled "Patented July 15, 1862; also in Europe 20 Dec. 1862." In addition she bears the label of her New York manufacturer, Joseph Lyon and Company. The patent for her design was held by Enoch Rice Morrison of New York City.

Another small doll pushes a baby carriage which is set in motion by winding the left rear wheel (fig. 34). The carriage is red with gilt decoration and is marked "W. F. Goodwin's Patents Jan'y 22, 1867 and Aug't 25th, 1868." The doll has a painted pressed-cloth head and jointed metal arms and legs which move as the carriage pulls her along, making her look as if she were walking. A more fortunate lady rides in her horse-drawn carriage, which at one time had a small figure of a boy hitching a ride behind her (fig. 35). She was made in the late nineteenth century by the Ives, Blakeslee, and Williams Company of Bridgeport, Connecticut. In their 1893 catalogue she was described as "Mechanical Horse with Old Lady Driver. . . . A large and very comical Toy. . . . The motion of the old lady driver is very perfect. She moves her body back and forth very naturally. No. 15-3 patented galloping horse 17″ long by 10″ high, price per dozen $33.00."

34. Doll and carriage, labelled "Wm. F. Goodwins, Patents Jan'y 22, 1867 and Aug't 25th, 1868;" h. 11 in., l. 12 in. (128,698).

33. *"Autoperipatetikos," or walking doll with decorated china head. Labeled "Patented July 15, 1862; also in Europe 20 Dec. 1862." Made by Joseph Lyon & Co., New York City; h. 10 in. (123,032).*

35. *"Mechanical Horse with Old Lady Driver," soldered-tin spring-wound toy, made by Ives, Blakeslee & Williams Co., Bridgeport, Connecticut, 1870-1890; h. 10 in., l. 17 in. (117,547).*

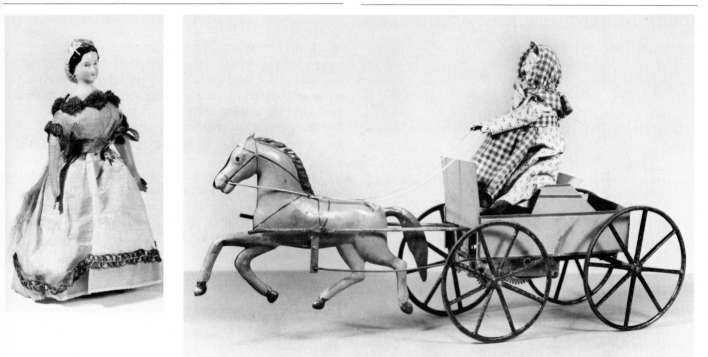

36. Children's toys and dolls' furniture as displayed in the Gardner-Pingree House. The painted bedroom set and the spool-turned bed both date about 1850-1875, while the chest-on-chest was probably specially made in the first quarter of the nineteenth century.

While dolls and their many accessories, including quantities of clothing and furniture (see figs. 30, 36), are almost exclusively the playthings of young girls, toys are objects of delight, amusement, and instruction for boys and girls of all ages. The doll factories of Germany, France, and England supplied most of the dolls played with in this country between 1840 and 1910. In contrast, however, most toys were American made. With the beginnings of the soldered-tin toy industry in Connecticut in the early 1840s and the development of cast-iron toys made in Connecticut, New York, Pennsylvania, and elsewhere during the Civil War era, American machine-manufactured toys dominated an ever-expanding market. Many patents were issued to toy inventors, and catalogues and advertisements were circulated in great quantities. The competition was as keen among manufacturers then as it is now for the newest mechanical gimmick or the latest model of a carriage, trolley, car, or boat that would sell.

The toys at the Essex Institute are largely from the collection that Mrs. Henry Goodwin Vaughan gave to the museum in 1946. Among them are early soldered-tin pull toys, tin mechanicals, wooden toys, and cast-iron models of a quality and rarity seldom seen by collectors today. As with the dolls in the Institute's collection, the toys have often been described and illustrated in the voluminous literature on toys.[10]

Many of the nineteenth-century American toys are concerned with various methods of transportation, since movement is implicit in a vehicle of almost any sort. A rowboat with a fully clothed oarsman is a particularly novel spring-wound toy since it actually worked when set in the water (fig. 37). Made by Ives and Company of Bridgeport, the oarsman moved the wooden oars attached to his hands, propelling the boat forward.

37. Rowboat and oarsman, soldered tin with cloth and wooden parts, made by Ives & Co., Bridgeport, Connecticut, 1870-1880; l. 11 in. (126,905a.247).

Most wheeled toys were models of horses and buggies, the predominant transportation method in the nineteenth century. A wooden horse pull toy (fig. 38), which is painted gray with a handsomely decorated green saddle blanket, was probably made in the early nineteenth century. Wooden toys were especially popular in the days before the industrial revolution, when it became possible to make hundreds of identical die-stamped metal toys. Horse-drawn coaches and wagons were also popular playthings, and a small, colorful wooden coach with two horses was "brought from Leghorn in 1804 by my brother Samuel Gray, S. R. Frothingham" according to an inscription on its original box (fig. 39).

A soldered-tin horse and wagon (fig. 40) with "Wells & Co. Express" stenciled on its bright red sides is far more within the American tradition of the mid-nineteenth century than the little coach from Leghorn, Italy. "Wells & Co." may refer to forerunners of the Wells Fargo company that helped to open the western frontier. While the maker of the toy cannot be positively identified, it is similar to an express wagon shown in plate 46 of *The George Brown Sketch Book* and may have been made by Brown.

38. *Horse pull toy, carved of wood and painted (wheels may be a later replacement), 1800-1840; h. 20 in., l. 16½ in. (109,831).*

39. *Coach and driver with its original box. According to inscription on the box cover it was brought from Leghorn, Italy, in 1804; coach h. 3 in., l. 8 in. (107,216).*

40. *"Wells & Co. Express" soldered-tin wagon pull toy drawn by two white horses, ca. 1860; h. 6 in., l. 20 in. (100,780).*

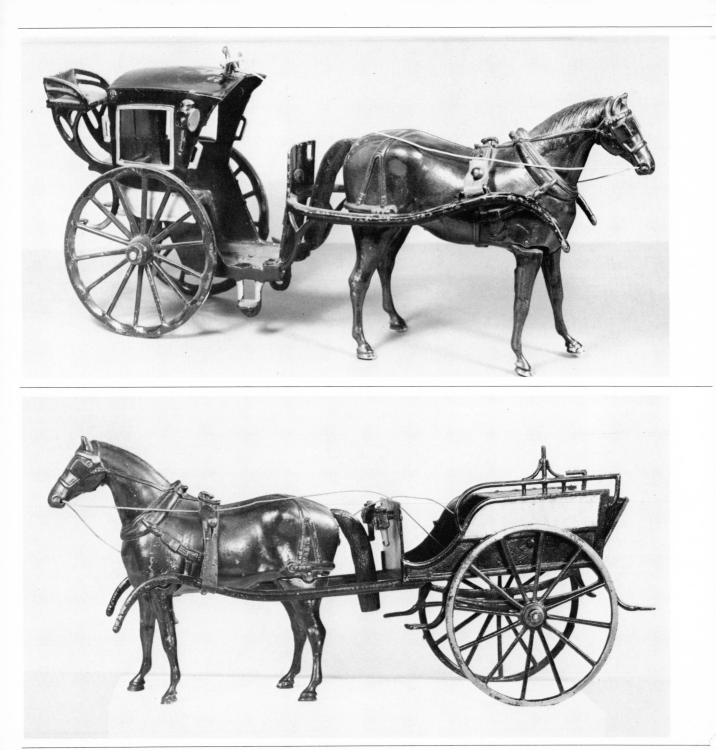

Two examples of more urbane methods of transportation are a horse-drawn hansom cab and a tilbury cart (figs. 41, 42), both cast-iron pull toys made by Ives and Company in the 1880s. Ives cast-iron toys are generally thought to be the finest and their detailing quite extraordinary, such as the moveable tailgate in the tilbury cart illustrated here. The horses in both of these toys are identical and they have pin joints at their shoulders so that when they are pulled across the floor they appear to be walking.

A large, wooden Victoria coach (fig. 43) has its horses mounted on a wheeled platform, and is beautifully finished in every detail. The wooden horses are covered with white fur to give them a more realistic look. The passenger seats are upholstered in gray silk, and the coach wheels have nicely turned brass hubcaps.

A coupé and dos-à-dos phaeton, cast-iron toys of about 1900-1910 (fig. 44) are not marked by their manufacturer so they cannot be positively identified. The phaeton has holes in the rear seat, indicating that some of the passenger figures are missing. The coupé is similar to coupé no. 77 in catalog number 16 of the Kenton Hardware Company, Kenton, Ohio.

In the nineteenth century good horses were much admired for their strength, speed, and good looks, and they were the essential means of transportation until the early decades of the twentieth century. Racing horses were also specially bred and pampered, much as they are now, and the young child who pulled a tin race horse with a once-smart jockey in his blue-and-yellow silks (fig. 45) could let his imagination travel fast and far to the races where the best horse was much prized. The childish imagination was catered to in a whimsical way as well by the toy manufacturers, as indicated by three small pull toys (fig. 46), one of which is drawn by a lion. A fanciful chariot pulled by three horses could take a child back to the Roman days that he later studied so thoroughly in his classroom Latin exercises. The pig cart has a bell mounted under the cart that rings with each revolution of the cart wheels; it was made by the Gong Bell Toy Company of East Hampton, Connecticut. The maker of the gladiator is unknown, but the lion and his chariot, made of soldered tin, are pictured in plate 23 of *The George Brown Sketch Book.*

44. Left, *dos-à-dos phaeton and* right, *coupé, both cast-iron pull toys of about 1900; l. 13 in. and 14 in. respectively (126,905a.43, .74).*

45. *Horse-and-jockey pull toy of soldered tin, 1870-1880; h. 15 in., l. 12½ in. (126,905a.70).*

46. *Three whimsical pull toys of the 1880-1900 period.* Top, *chariot drawn by a lion, soldered tin; l. 6½ in. (126,9052.180,.194,.183);* Center, *pig cart, cast iron, made by the Gong Bell Toy Co., East Hampton, Conn.; l. 6½ in.;* Bottom, *chariot and horses, cast iron; l. 12 in.*

47. Left, *mechanical steam pumper, soldered tin; h. 7½ in., l. 15 in.* Right, *hose reel, soldered tin; h. 8 in., l. 10½ in. Both pull toys were sold by Althof, Bergmann & Co., New York, between 1870 and 1880 (126,905a.188, .195).*

Fire equipment was very colorful, and there was much ceremony and importance attached to fire companies, especially as the urban areas of America grew rapidly during the nineteenth century. Two pieces of equipment, a mechanical steam pumper and a hose reel (fig. 47) were made by Althof Bergmann and Company of New York in the 1870s and 1880s. The spring-wound steam pumper, which has a bell that rings as it is pulled across the floor, demonstrates the growth of mechanical technology since the days of the bucket brigade. Both vehicles were once brightly painted, and no doubt sales of such toys as these were boosted by the heroic reports of the great city fires, particularly in Chicago and Boston, during the last half of the century.

With the invention of the steam engine, methods of mass transportation were developed, and small toy models of trains and various engine-powered boats appeared on the market, especially after the Civil War period. A homemade wooden model of the Eastern Railroad Station in Salem (fig. 48) was created sometime in the 1830s, with a wooden steam engine labeled "Naumkeag" and a flatcar. The turntable was once surrounded by a platform which had a wheeled screw device for rotating the engine on the table.

48. *Model of the Eastern Railroad Station, Salem, 1830-1840, pine; building h. 13½ in., l. 16½ in. (117,714).*

An early trackless tin locomotive (fig. 49) has cars that are stencil-labeled "New York" and "Boston." The engine was made by George W. Brown and Company of Forestville, Connecticut in the 1860s, and they probably made the cars as well. Toy trains running on tracks were a later innovation. The wheels of the side-wheeler "Baltic" were actually put to use on the floor and a third small wheel was put under the stern to help the ship move along as it was pulled (fig. 50). The soldered-tin ship lacks the authentic details of the "New York" (fig. 51), but the rhythm of its stamped-and-painted decorations gives it a very nautical profile. The "New York" has a realistic-looking deck house, air ventilators, smoke stacks, and most of her original flags flying. Her side wheels are able to propel the boat in the water after being wound with a key. The "New York" was made in Germany by the Maerklin Company for the American trade about 1890. She is a handsome miniature of the many steamships that navigated the rivers of nineteenth-century America, providing an indispensable means of passenger and commercial transportation.

Three wooden toy groups, also made in Germany, probably in the first half of the nineteenth century, represent the European tradition of toy making at its best. For centuries craftsmen in the Oberammergau area of Germany made finely detailed carved-and-painted wooden toys. Some craftsmen emigrated to Pennsylvania in the eighteenth and nineteenth centuries, so attribution of some toys, such as the Noah's Ark (fig. 52), is difficult to make. The Noah's Ark has been widely published, and it travelled with *The Flowering of American Folk Art* organized by the Whitney Museum of American Art in 1974.[11] American collectors and art historians look at the Noah's Ark today with a different view than that which was originally intended: as folk art it has transcended its use as a child's plaything with its moral instruction implicit in its form.

---

52. *Noah's Ark, painted wooden figures and boat, probably made in Pennsylvania ca. 1800-1850. The ark has fifty-five pairs of animals (not all illustrated) including a unicorn and his mate. Dimensions of ark: h. 8 in., w. 17 in., d. 5½ in. (108,643).*

Of more obvious European origin are a toy spice-and-sweet shop and a village at harvest time (figs. 53, 54). The walled village has brightly painted peasant figures, most of whom are holding farming tools, and several Germanic-style buildings including a town hall and a church. At one time there were probably more buildings or walls, as the blocks do not perfectly match up. The "Spezerei Handlung" is a perfect miniature version of a real shop in every detail: glass shop windows, painted-tile floors with marbleized entry steps, painted grained drawers, each with its own paper label. The little jugs and bottles on the top shelf are even labeled as to their contents, for instance "Marzepand," and the little china-headed doll shopkeeper holds a package ready to go for a customer. Models of other shops were made — dry goods, groceries, butcher shops, or pharmacies — and no doubt many young children enjoyed practicing their commercial skills as they played with these miniature rooms.

54. *Village at harvest time, one of an infinite variety of toy villages made in the Nuremberg area of Germany. Early nineteenth century, wood painted with watercolor; figures h. 2½ to 3 in., church h. 8½ in. (108,644).*

53. *"Spezerei Handlung," a German spice-and-sweet shop, second half of the nineteenth century; h. 13 in., w. 18 in., d. 9¾ in. (100,784).*

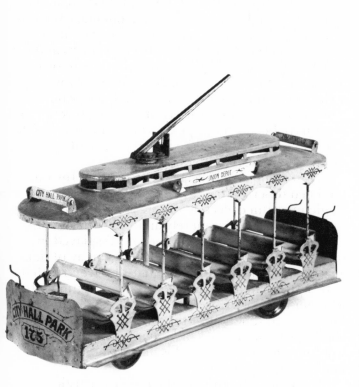

The dolls and toys in the Essex Institute collections are representative of those used by children in New England from the early nineteenth century through the earliest decades of the twentieth century. As we have seen, most of the toys in the 1840-1910 period were made commercially, and it therefore seems appropriate to conclude this history with examples of metal toys that represented the latest methods of transportation at the turn of the century. A horse-drawn omnibus of soldered tin is brightly stenciled with red-on-yellow floral decorations and is labeled with the route "Broadway & 4th Avenue" (fig. 55). Vehicles of this kind were probably among the last to give way to the trolley (which was at first horse-drawn) and the automobile. George W. Brown and Company of Forestville, Connecticut, has created a realistic spring-wound toy with two galloping horses, driver, and a back door that opens on hinges. The bus has seats for its passengers. The trolley car (fig. 56) has passenger seats that can be flipped over with a reversal in direction. The signs "City Hall Park" and "Union Depot" also reverse, as does the trolley line hookup when the open car heads back to its imaginary destination. The trolley car was made by the Morton E. Converse Company of Winchendon, Massachusetts, which made another version as a pull toy, without the spring-wound motor. Converse also supplied the body of this trolley to the Lionel Electric Train Company. Lionel mounted the body on a four-wheeled chassis which ran on a 2⅞ inch-gauge track.

Three versions of Ford's early model cars represent the only concession of the Essex Institute collections to twentieth-century transportation (fig. 57). Made of pressed steel, lithographed tin, and cast iron (left to right) the cars are documentary records of how the real automobile appeared when it first moved uncertainly across the dirt cart tracks and city cobblestones of early twentieth-century America. These car models are as eagerly sought by toy collectors as the real cars are by antique car buffs. They were made by a variety of manufacturers[12] and must have been very popular with young boys of the era who could imagine the new romance of mechanized speed in their vehicles.

The toy and doll collection at the Essex Institute has been described as "what is perhaps the finest single museum collection of toys in America,"[13] and this booklet provides merely an introduction to the charm and variety of the collection. Displayed in several different exhibition areas, the array of dolls and toys and their accessories must be seen firsthand to be appreciated and enjoyed. The museum visitor, whether a serious collector, a casual daydreamer indulging in fantasies of the past, or an intrigued child to whom the days of long ago are a mystery, will find plenty to engage his imagination or his knowledge.

Not all dolls and toys of the past are artistic creations, but it is fortunate that the crude and the beautiful, the handmade and the machine-manufactured, have been saved by collectors after the playthings have outlived their original usefulness. Eventually the best of collected material gravitates to museums, either by purchase, by gift of original owners or their families, or by collectors whose generosity has made possible the acquisition of these priceless mementoes of childhood. The Essex Institute has been the fortunate beneficiary of past friends and contributors, and we hope that our fine collection of toys and dolls will continue to attract future generations of interested visitors, donors, and collectors.

57. Left, *Ford Model T coupé of pressed steel, part of the "Buddy L" toy line made by the Moline Pressed Steel Co., East Moline, Illinois, 1916-1922; h. 6¾ in., l. 11 in.* Center, *Ford Model A, made of lithographed tin and manufactured by the Upton Machine Co., St. Joseph, Michigan, 1929; h. 3½ in., l. 7 in.* Right, *cast-iron Ford Model T, made by the Arcade Manufacturing Co., Freeport, Illinois, ca. 1920; h. 4 in., l. 5 in. (126,905a.27, .71, .30).*

BIBLIOGRAPHY

Althof, Bergmann Co. *Reprint of 1874 Catalog.* Philadelphia: Antique Toy Collectors of America.

Barenholtz, Edith F., ed. *The George Brown Sketchbook.* Princeton: Pyne Press, 1971.

Coleman, Dorothy S., Elizabeth A., and Evelyn J. *The Collector's Encyclopedia of Dolls.* New York: Crown Publishers, 1968.

Coleman, Evelyn, Elizabeth, and Dorothy. *The Age of Dolls.* Washington, D. C.: 1965.

Cranmer, Daniel. *Cast Iron and Tin Toys of Yesterday.* Gas City, Indiana: L-W Promotions, 1974.

Culff, Robert. *The World of Toys.* London: Hamlyn Press, 1969. Doll Collectors of America. *Doll Collectors Manual.* Warner, N.H.: Mayflower Press, 1964, 1967.

Early, Alice K. *English Dolls, Effigies and Puppets.* London: B. T. Batsford, 1955.

Fawcett, Clara Hallard. *Dolls, A Guide for Collectors.* New York: H. L. Lindquist Publications, 1947.

Foley, Daniel. *Toys Through the Ages.* New York: Chilton Press, 1962.

Fox, Carl. *The Doll.* New York: Harry N. Abrams Pub., 1974.

Fraser, Antonia. *A History of Toys.* London: Delacorte Press, 1966.

Freeman, Ruth and Larry. *Cavalcade of Toys.* New York: Century House, 1942.

Gerken, Jo Elizabeth. *Wonderful Dolls of Papier Mache.* Lincoln, Nebraska: Union College Press, 1970.

Gerken, Jo Elizabeth. *Wonderful Dolls of Wax.* Lincoln, Nebraska: Doll Research Associates, 1964.

Hertz, Louis H. *Riding the Tin Plate Rails.* Wethersfield, Conn.: Mark Haber & Co., 1944.

Hertz, Louis H. *Collecting Model Trains.* New York: Simmons-Boardman Co., 1956.

Hertz, Louis H. *Messrs. Ives of Bridgeport.* Wethersfield, Conn.: Mark Haber & Co., 1950.

Hertz, Louis, H. *Handbook of American Toys.* Wethersfield, Conn.: Mark Haber & Co., 1950.

Hertz, Louis H. *The Toy Collector.* New York: Funk and Wagnalls Co., 1969.

Hillier, Mary. *Pageant of Toys.* New York: Taplinger Publishing Co., 1965.

Hillier, Mary. *Dolls and Doll Makers.* New York: G. P. Putnam's Sons, 1968.

Johl, Janet Pagler. *Your Dolls and Mine.* New York: H. L. Lindquist Publications, 1952.

McClintock, Inez and Marshall. *Toys In America.* Washington, D. C.: Public Affairs Press, 1961.

McClinton, Katherine. *Antiques of American Childhood.* New York: Potter Press, 1970.

Merrill, Madeline O. and **Perkins,** Nellie W. *Handbook of Collectible Dolls,* Vols. 1, 2, 3. Melrose, Mass.: Woodward & Miller, 1969-1974.

Noble, John. *A Treasury of Beautiful Dolls.* New York: Hawthorne Books, 1971.

Perelman, Leon J. *Perelman Antique Toy Museum.* Philadelphia: Leon J. Perelman, 1972.

Remise, J., and **Fondin,** J. *The Golden Age of Toys.* S. A. Lausanne, Switzerland: Edita Press, 1969.

Schroeder, Joseph J. Jr. *Toys, Games, and Dolls.* Chicago: Follet Publishing Co., 1971.

Von Boehn, Max. *Dolls and Puppets.* Boston: Charles T. Bransford Co., Revised edition 1956.

NOTES

1. See the following publications arranged in chronological order: Alice Van Leer Carrick, "Playthings of the Past," *The Magazine Antiques* 1 (1922): 10-16. Ella Shannon Bowles, "Dolls of Old New England," *The Antiquarian* 6 (1926): 8-12, 26. Ruth P. Cole, "Dolls at the Essex Institute, Salem, Massachusetts," *Hobbies,* The Magazine for Collectors 42 (1938): 26-7. Janet Pagter Johl, *Your Dolls and Mine* (New York: H. L. Lindquist Publications, 1952). Dan Foley, *Toys Through the Ages* (Philadelphia: Chilton Books, 1962). Carl Fox, *The Doll* (New York: Harry N. Abrams Inc., 1974). *The Craftsman in America* (National Geographic Society, 1975).

2. Quoted in Foley, *Toys Through the Ages,* p. 29.

3. Madeline O. Merrill and Nellie W. Perkins, *Handbook of Collectible Dolls,* 3 vols. (Melrose, Mass.: Woodward & Miller, 1969-1974), 3:224 E.

4. Illustrated in Fox, *The Doll,* plates 62, 32 respectively.

5. Fox, *The Doll,* plate 79.

6. Fox, *The Doll,* plate 137.

7. Merrill and Perkins, *Handbook,* 2:118 H.

8. Merrill and Perkins, *Handbook,* 3:194 B.

9. Merrill and Perkins, *Handbook,* 3:206 A.

10. For instance, Foley, *Toys Through the Ages;* Inez and Marshall McClintock, *Toys in America* (Washington, D.C.: Public Affairs Press, 1961.)

11. Jean Lipman and Alice Winchester, *The Flowering of American Folk Art 1776-1876* (New York: The Viking Press, 1974) p. 179.

12. See Dan Cranmer, *Cast Iron and Tin Toys of Yesterday* (Gas City, Indiana: L-W Promotions, 1974) p. 49, 61; Leon J. Perelman, *Perelman Antique Toy Museum* (Philadelphia: Leon J. Perelman, 1972).

13. Ruth and Larry Freeman, *Cavalcade of Toys* (New York: Century House, 1942) p. 390.